A CALL TO
GROWTH

A CALL TO
GROWTH

ESTABLISHING THE
GROWING BELIEVER

DR. BILLIE HANKS, JR.

INTERNATIONAL EVANGELISM ASSOCIATION
SALADO, TEXAS 76571

For more information about this ministry, write or call:

INTERNATIONAL EVANGELISM ASSOCIATION
PO BOX 1174
SALADO, TEXAS 76571 - 1174
(254) 947-3030

Or visit us on the World Wide Web at WWW.IEAOM.ORG

Printed in the United States of America

This book is
dedicated
to those who share
the vision of
Spiritual Multiplication.

CONTENTS

ACKNOWLEGEMENTS

"If you love Me. . . feed My lambs." (John 21:15)

A Call To Growth has involved five years of writing, field testing, and work on the part of many people who have prayerfully refined these intermediate level materials on Christ-centered spiritual relationships.

To the team of writers and other close friends who have lived this message and sought to share it with others, goes my deepest gratitude.

Without the editing and discipling skills of Dr. Bill Shell, the early coordination of Rev. Sam Cook, the literary and creative gifts of Rev. Dan Nelson and Mr. Walt Wooden, and the design and typesetting skills of Mr. Randy Ray, *A Call To Growth* would never have moved from concept to reality.

Randy Craig's enthusiastic lay leadership, Dr. Tim Beougher's textual research, Max Barnett's Biblical studies, Wayne Watts' inspirational writing, and the assistance of IEA's dedicated staff and interns have all been orchestrated by the Lord to produce *A Call To Growth*.

We are especially grateful for the pioneering pastors and churches who have helped refine this new process of assimilation during the years of field testing.

Collectively, we seek one common goal:
To see God's people personally *grow* and *multiply* as they share their faith in Christ!

"Go therefore and make disciples. . . teaching them to observe all that I have commanded you." (Matthew 28:19 & 20)

Billie Hanks, Jr.

DISCIPLER'S GUIDE INTRODUCTION

USING *A CALL TO GROWTH*

A Call to Growth is designed to enable you to continue encouraging new believers and new members in their basic spiritual disciplines.

CONTENTS OF *A CALL TO GROWTH*:

The Discipler's Packet:

Discipler's Guide

Timothy's Guide

Spiritual Journal

Scripture Memory Card Holder

The Timothy's Packet:

Timothy's Guide

Spiritual Journal

Scripture Memory Card Holder

EXPLANATION OF TERMS

NOTE: In this material, the Discipler and the Timothy will be referred to as "he," "him," and "his." The generic use of these pronouns refer to *both* male and female.

A. **Discipler**—A Christian who is growing consistently in his relationship with Christ and is showing a younger believer how to mature in the faith and share it naturally (Matthew 4:19).

B. **Timothy**—A Christian who is seeking to grow spiritually by spending time with and observing the example of a more experienced Christian. This equipping principle is derived from the New Testament example of Paul who *taught* and *trained* a growing young believer named Timothy (see Acts 16:1-3 and 2 Timothy 2:2).

    NOTE: For best results, we recommend that men disciple men and women disciple women. An enjoyable Christ-centered friendship is the *short*-term spiritual objective. A victorious life with natural spiritual reproduction is the *long*-term objective.

C. **Session**—A period of 60 to 90 minutes during which a Timothy meets with his Discipler for Christian fellowship and spiritual instruction. Including the initial meeting, *A Call To Growth* is normally completed in 11 to 15 weeks. The completion rate should be based on the individual needs of your Timothy.

D. **Weekly Spiritual Growth Assignments**—Inspirational activities designed for both you and your Timothy to complete between your scheduled sessions. These assignments are printed in your Discipler's Guide and in the Timothy's Guide.

MEETING WITH YOUR TIMOTHY

A. This material is designed to help you be spiritually prepared for each session with your Timothy.

B. Your Timothy will experience rich personal fellowship with God through his weekly assignments. These assignments consist of sermon note-taking, daily quiet times, Bible study, Scripture memorization, plus inspirational reading on prayer, evangelism, and the joy of giving.

C. *A Call To Growth* also includes *Spiritual Application Projects*. These projects provide the opportunity for you and your Timothy to enjoy practical ministry activities together so you can apply the principles being taught. Five projects are listed beginning on page 65. These activities are designed for field experience in evangelism. Choose only four of the five projects to use during *A Call To Growth*. You may prayerfully determine both the sequence and the selection of projects based upon the needs of your Timothy.

D. To answer your Timothy's questions and provide quality spiritual guidance, you should plan to stay at least two weeks *ahead* in these materials. Covenant with yourself to spend enough time in prayer to arrive at each session with a *prepared* heart and mind!

E. Your Timothy will sometimes have questions about selected portions of Scripture. These questions will be important to him, so relax, and take the necessary time to answer each one of them. If you do not know the answer, you can say, "I don't know, but I will try to find out and discuss this with you next week." Be sure to make note of his question. Your pastor or Bible teacher will usually be happy to serve as a resource person.

F. If you are unable to meet with your Timothy due to a schedule conflict or an unexpected problem, simply meet together at another mutually agreeable time during the following week. Seek to be *consistent,* yet *flexible,* and slow down if your Timothy has personal needs that require extra prayer and discussion. Remember that covering these lessons at the suggested completion rate is second in priority to successfully meeting the spiritual needs of your Timothy. Try to schedule your meetings with a flexible ending time, so both of you can be relaxed and enjoy the session together.

YOUR MINISTRY AS A DISCIPLER

A. As a Discipler, you will be demonstrating the process of personal growth by modeling the following spiritual disciplines:

1. **Sermon Note-taking.**
2. **Daily Quiet Time and Prayer.**
3. **Personal Bible Study.**
4. **Scripture Memory.**
5. **Meditation on Memory Verses.**
6. **Natural Lifestyle Evangelism.**

B. Since you will be teaching your Timothy by example, it will be important for you to demonstrate the use of the *Spiritual Journal* (see the journal for instructions). A *Quiet Time Reading Guide* is located in Appendix A of the Timothy's Guide. It is specifically designed for ease of application. You and your Timothy do *not* need to read the same passages in order to exchange Quiet Time insights each week.

C. In *A Call To Growth* your primary objective is to encourage your Timothy's long-term spiritual development. Your task will be to assist him as he builds his *own convictions* about the personal disciplines being taught during these sessions. He will need to learn that they are the key to his sustained spiritual progress!

D. Avoid merely asking your Timothy to *do* assignments. Encour-
    age him to personally discover the spiritual purpose behind each
    new step. Point out that *understanding* with *application*
    leads to a godly character!

INITIAL MEETING DISCIPLER'S PREPARATION MATERIAL

"And let us consider how to stimulate one another to love and good deeds." (Hebrews 10:24)

PERSONAL FELLOWSHIP (10-15 minutes).

If you studied *A Call To Joy* together, begin by briefly reviewing how God has used those weeks in his life. Concentrate on being a *good listener* during your meetings.

If this is your *first* meeting together, begin by getting acquainted and briefly talking about subjects like – family, occupation, school, personal interests, and favorite recreational activities. Your Timothy needs to realize that you want to establish a genuine friendship. Seek to learn where your Timothy *is* in terms of his spiritual development, and where he would like to be in the future.

Exchange personal testimonies of conversion. If you detect a *lack* of clarity, open the "Bridge Illustration" booklet, and slowly read, explaining and discussing each verse. Next, ask him where he is on the bridge and seek to pray the sinner's prayer.

PRESENT YOUR SPIRITUAL OBJECTIVES (30 minutes).

- Briefly preview the Timothy's Guide and explain it's format. Show him the *Weekly Spiritual Growth Assignments, Inspirational Reading Section, Lessons In Christian Discipleship*, and the Appendix.

- Explain that the *Inspirational Reading Section* is composed of excerpts from three books: *If You Love Me, Everyday Evangelism*, and *The Gift of Giving.* These chapters focus on the five kinds of prayer taught in the Bible, three natural approaches to personal witness, and the Biblical pattern for giving.

- Discuss the value of meeting together and mutual accountability.

- Review the use of the *Spiritual Journal* by discussing page 6 in the Journal. Next, read the first Quiet Time (Appendix A) and actually do a sample Quiet Time together using your *Spiritual Journals.*

- Discuss several reasons why some Christians miss the blessing of having a daily Quiet Time.

  > *"And others are the ones on whom seed was sown among the thorns; these are the ones who have heard the word, and the worries of the world, and the deceitfulness of riches, and the desires for other things enter in and choke the word, and it becomes unfruitful."* (Mark 4:18 & 19)

- Remind your Timothy that lasting spiritual growth will take place as he *yields* himself to Christ and disciplines himself to seek God's will in every decision. Pause to emphasize this verse *"...discipline yourself for the purpose of godliness."* (1 Timothy 4:7c) Next, discuss possible changes that need to occur in his weekly schedule in order to give priority to spiritual growth.

• Challenge him to consider the importance of daily Quiet Time reading in the light of this verse; King David once said, *"In the morning, O Lord, Thou wilt hear my voice; In the morning I will order my prayer to Thee and eagerly watch."* (Psalm 5:3)

BIBLE STUDY (40 Minutes).

• Explain that temptation is an ongoing battle in the Christian life. Turn to page 59 and lead your Timothy through the Bible study, *Dealing with Temptation.*

PRAYER TIME TOGETHER

You can —
• *thank* the Lord for the opportunity of meeting together.
• *ask* Him to build your friendship!
• *praise* Him for His activity in your lives.

GLOSSARY FOR ALL SESSIONS:

DG = *A Call To Growth* Discipler's Guide
TG = *A Call To Growth* Timothy's Guide
LCD = *Lessons in Christian Discipleship*
        (located on page 141 of your Timothy's Guide).
SJ = *Spiritual Journal*
SM = Scripture Memory Verses
QT = Quiet Time
SN = Sermon Notes

WEEKLY SPIRITUAL GROWTH ASSIGNMENT #1
(5-10 minutes).

NOTE: Both you and your Timothy will complete the same assignments each week. Plan to stay at least two weeks ahead.

1. Start enjoying daily QTs using your *Quiet Time Reading Guide* in Appendix A, page 231 in your Timothy's Guide. Be prepared to share your favorite personal insights next week. (If you, as a Discipler, are on a different QT reading schedule, you may continue using that plan).

2. Take sermon notes using your SJ. Be prepared to review highlights during your next meeting.

3. Memorize **Romans 3:23** along with its heading, *All Have Sinned*. It will be helpful if you both memorize using the same translation. Remember to quote the reference before and after each verse. Be prepared to share your verse next week. (As a Discipler, you may have already memorized the assigned verses. If so, this will be an excellent time for review, so be prepared to quote each week's verse). (Verse cards are located at the back of your TG).

4. Read the introduction and complete Lesson 1 in the LCD located on page 145 of your Timothy's Guide.

5. Read TG Chapter 1, *Adoration*. Mark meaningful highlights, and come prepared to discuss them next week.

NOTE: Remind your Timothy to always bring his Bible, study materials, and a pen or pencil to each meeting. Make a mutual commitment to arrive and leave on time and to be at every session unless providentially hindered.

SESSION ONE DISCIPLER'S PREPARATION MATERIAL

"And I give eternal life to them, and they shall never perish; and no one shall snatch them out of my hand. My Father, who has given them to Me, is greater than all; and no one is able to snatch them out of the Father's hand." (John 10:28 & 29)

PERSONAL FELLOWSHIP (5-10 Minutes).

Use this unstructured time to continue building your friendship. Seek to communicate your genuine interest in your Timothy's life by asking about his activities during the past week. As it seems natural, move toward subjects that have *spiritual* significance (such as lessons learned, prayers answered, and the gospel shared).

SHARING FROM YOUR SPIRITUAL JOURNALS
(10-15 Minutes).

A. Exchange insights from your SJ—QT and SN highlights.

B. Share your SM verse with one another. Read and discuss
    Appendix B, *Scripture Memory*. (Appendix B is located in your
    TG, page 235).

BIBLE STUDY DISCUSSION (15-20 Minutes).

Review LCD, Lesson 1, *The New Relationship*. Remember to focus
on the meditation sections as you discuss this week's new insights.

CHRISTIAN MEDITATION (5 Minutes).

Take turns reading Appendix C aloud. Emphasize and discuss
points of special interest. (Appendix C is located in your TG, page
239).

TOPICAL READING DISCUSSION (10-15 Minutes).

Discuss TG, Chapter 1, *Adoration* highlights. Supplement your
discussion with page 9 in your *Spiritual Journal*.

PRAYER TIME TOGETHER (10-15 Minutes).

 Individually list *five* major attributes of God that cause you to love
and honor Him. Then take turns offering personal prayers of adoration to the Lord.

WEEKLY SPIRITUAL GROWTH ASSIGNMENT #2
(5-10 Minutes).

1. Pray to be an empowered witness each day this week!
2. Continue your daily QTs using the *Quiet Time Reading Guide*
    (Appendix A). Be prepared to share your favorite personal
    insights next week.
3. Take sermon notes using your SJ. Be prepared to review high-
    lights during your next meeting.

4. Memorize **ROMANS 6:23** along with its heading, *Sin Earns Spiritual Death*. Meditate on the meaning of this verse. Be prepared to share your verses next week.
5. Complete Lesson 2 in the LCD.
6. Read TG, Chapter 2, *Evangelism Flows Out of a Godly Life*. Mark meaningful highlights and come prepared to discuss them next week.

SESSION TWO DISCIPLER'S PREPARATION MATERIAL

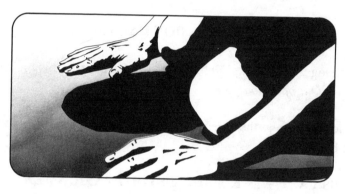

"But seek first His kingdom and His righteousness; and all these things shall be added to you." (Matthew 6:33)

SPIRITUAL APPLICATION PROJECT

Plan now to carry out a selected *Spiritual Application Project*, (page 65). You may wish to complete the project and Session 2 on the same night, or you can schedule Session 2 and the project on separate nights.

PERSONAL FELLOWSHIP (5-10 Minutes).

Ask your Timothy to share some of his experiences from the past week. Pay special attention to anything that he might say or imply about relationships with family, friends, or work associates. Remember that the primary purpose of your time together is sincerely meeting his individual spiritual needs, not just "covering" the assigned material.

SHARING FROM YOUR SPIRITUAL JOURNAL
(15-20 Minutes).

A. Exchange insights from your SJ—QT and SN highlights.

B. Share your two current SM verses.

TOPICAL READING DISCUSSION (15-25 Minutes).

A. Exchange favorite highlights from TG, Chapter 2, *Evangelism Flows Out of a Godly Life.*

B. Read and discuss the *Spiritual Overflow Illustration* in Appendix D.

DISCUSS LAST WEEK'S BIBLE STUDY ASSIGNMENT
(15-20 Minutes).

A. Review your LCD, Lesson 2, *Putting Christ First.* This is a very important chapter, because it is at the very heart of discipleship. To live the Spirit-filled life and to share the gospel effectively, we must give Jesus Christ first priority in all areas of our life.

B. Try to make certain that a sincere commitment to Christ's lordship is genuinely understood.

PRAYER TIME TOGETHER:

You can —
* *ask* the Lord for increased personal purity; considering your tongue, eyes, mind, hands, and heart.
* *commit* yourself to put Christ first in every area of your life.
* *ask* the Lord to give you increased discipline for spiritual growth so you can witness out of the overflow of His life within you.

WEEKLY SPIRITUAL GROWTH ASSIGNMENT #3
(5 Minutes).

1. Continue your daily QTs, praying to be an empowered witness! Be prepared to share your favorite personal insights next week.
2. Take sermon notes using your SJ. Be prepared to review highlights during your next meeting.
3. Memorize **HEBREWS 9:27** along with its heading, *All Die Physically*. Meditate on the meaning of this verse. Be prepared to share your verses next week.
4. Complete Lesson 3 in the LCD.
5. Read TG, Chapter 3, *Sharing a Word of Truth*. Mark meaningful highlights and come prepared to discuss them next week.

> During this coming week, prayerfully plan to meet together and complete the *Spiritual Application Project* of your choice. (page 65)

SESSION THREE DISCIPLER'S PREPARATION MATERIAL

"And you also were included in Christ when you heard the word of truth, the gospel of your salvation. Having believed, you were marked in Him with a seal, the promised Holy Spirit."
(Ephesians 1:13, NIV)

PERSONAL FELLOWSHIP (5-10 Minutes).

Ask your Timothy to share his best and worst experience of the past week. Briefly share one of your own spiritual victories or struggles. Be sensitive to the difficulties he might be having. Remember that building a Christ-centered friendship takes openness and genuine concern.

SHARING FROM YOUR SPIRITUAL JOURNALS
(15-20 Minutes).

A. Exchange favorite insights from your SJ – QT and SN high-
    lights.

B. Share your previous SM verses and discuss any new insights
    you may have received from learning these verses.

C. Read Appendix E aloud, stopping for comments and discussion.

TOPICAL READING DISCUSSION (15-25 Minutes).

Discuss TG, Chapter 3, *Sharing a Word of Truth* highlights. Exchange examples and practical opportunities for sharing a word of
truth in normal daily experience.

BIBLE STUDY DISCUSSION (15-20 Minutes).

Review your LCD, Lesson 3, *The Devotional Life*.

PRAYER TIME TOGETHER (5-10 Minutes).

Take turns praying for opportunities to share a word of truth this
next week. In addition, mention two non-Christian friends or relatives, and pray together for their conviction and conversion. Ask the
Lord to use both of you in any way He chooses in order to help bring
this to pass.

WEEKLY SPIRITUAL GROWTH ASSIGNMENT #4
(5 Minutes).

1. Share at least one word of truth with someone this week.
2. Continue your daily QTs, praying to be an empowered witness!
    Be prepared to share your favorite personal insights next week.
3. Take sermon notes using your SJ. Be prepared to review high-
    lights during your next meeting.

4. Memorize **ROMANS 5:8** along with its heading, *Christ Died For Us While We Were Still Sinners.* Meditate on the deep meaning of this important verse. Be prepared to share your verses next week.

5. Complete Lesson 4 in the LCD.

6. Read TG, Chapter 4, *Intercession.* Mark meaningful highlights and come prepared to discuss them next week.

SESSION FOUR DISCIPLER'S PREPARATION MATERIAL

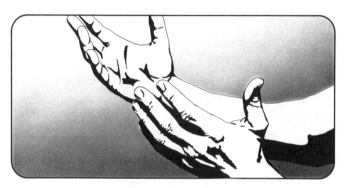

"We always thank God for all of you, mentioning you in our prayers. We continually remember before our God and Father your work produced by faith, your labor prompted by love, and your endurance inspired by hope in our Lord Jesus Christ."
(1 Thessalonians 1:2-3, NIV)

PERSONAL FELLOWSHIP (5-10 Minutes).

Continue to enjoy building your friendship as you meet together weekly. Focus on what God has been doing in your lives this week!

SHARING FROM YOUR SPIRITUAL JOURNALS
(15-20 Minutes).

A. Exchange insights from your SJ—QT and SN highlights.

B. Share your previous SM verses and discuss the insights you received while meditating on your new memory verse.

C. Compare experiences of sharing a word of truth this past week.

BIBLE STUDY DISCUSSION (15-20 Minutes).

Discuss your LCD, Lesson 4, Prayer—*Evidence of Dependency.*

TOPICAL READING DISCUSSION (15-25 Minutes).

Discuss the highlights of TG, Chapter 4, *Intercession.* Supplement your discussion with page 13 in your *Spiritual Journal.* Take a few minutes to review these sample Prayers of Intercession, then actually pray for several people with specific needs.

Lord, please —

- help _____ to . . .
- strengthen _____ for . . .
- show _____ how much . . .
- heal _____ if it is . . .
- use _____ to . . .
- cause _____ to . . .
- provide _____ with . . .

PRAYER TIME TOGETHER (5-10 Minutes).

List two or three specific requests for individuals in the daily prayer portion of your *Spiritual Journal* (page 14). In addition, select one or more family members, ministries, lost friends, or government representatives to pray for on different days of the week. Write their names in the Intercession section of your *Spiritual Journal.* Agree to pray together for several specific intercessory needs.

WEEKLY SPIRITUAL GROWTH ASSIGNMENT #5
(5 Minutes).

1. Continue your daily QTs, praying to be an empowered witness! Be prepared to share your favorite personal insights next week.
2. Take sermon notes using your SJ. Be prepared to review high-lights during your next meeting.
3. Memorize **EPHESIANS 2:8 & 9** along with its heading, *By God's Love We Are Saved Through Faith.* Meditate on the meaning of this verse. Be prepared to share your verses next week.
4. Complete Lesson 5 in the LCD.
5. Read TG, Chapter 5, *Sharing Your Testimony.* Mark meaningful highlights and come prepared to discuss them next week. Be sure to complete the *My Personal Testimony* section.

During this coming week, prayerfully plan to meet together and complete the *Spiritual Application Project* of your choice.

SESSION FIVE DISCIPLER'S PREPARATION MATERIAL

". . . He has committed to us the message of reconciliation."
(2 Corinthians 5:19c, NIV)

PERSONAL FELLOWSHIP (5-10 Minutes).

SHARING FROM YOUR SPIRITUAL JOURNALS
(15-20 Minutes).

A. Exchange insights from your SJ—QT and SN highlights.

B. Share your previous SM verses and discuss any insights you received from meditating on this week's new verse.

DISCUSS BEING A RESTED WITNESS

Read 1 Corinthians 3:16 with your Timothy, *"Do you not know that you are a temple of God, and that the Spirit of God dwells in you?"* Point out that many Christians stay up too late at night and never get enough rest. We each have to take care of our own temples. We often become too tired to even think of sharing a witness or ministering to others. When this happens, we simply end up trying to make it through the day! Discuss your physical requirements and decide how much sleep you need, then make the needed changes to be your very best. We only have a limited number of days to serve, so let's make each one count for Christ!

TOPICAL READING DISCUSSION (15-25 Minutes).

Discuss highlights from TG, Chapter 5, *Sharing Your Testimony.* Next, exchange brief personal testimonies with one another. In a supportive manner, seek to improve each other's content and pre-sentation. Make sure you emphasize the reason *why* you became a Christian.

BIBLE STUDY DISCUSSION (15-20 Minutes).

Review your LCD, Lesson 5, *Sharing Christ with Others.*

PRAYER TIME TOGETHER (5-10 Minutes).

Take turns praying about personal needs, plus opportunities to share your testimonies this week.

WEEKLY SPIRITUAL GROWTH ASSIGNMENT #6
(5 Minutes).

1. Practice sharing your personal testimony with two or more friends this week.
2. Continue your daily QTs, praying to be an empowered witness. Be prepared to share your favorite personal insights next week.

3. Take sermon notes using your SJ. Be prepared to review highlights during your next meeting.

4. Memorize **JOHN 1:12** along with its heading, *Believe and Receive*. Meditate on the meaning of this verse. Be prepared to share your verses next week.

5. Complete Lesson 6 in the LCD.

6. Read TG, Chapter 6, *Confession*. Mark meaningful highlights and come prepared to discuss them next week.

SESSION SIX
DISCIPLER'S
PREPARATION
MATERIAL

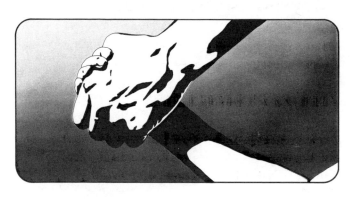

*"If we confess our sins, He is faithful and just and will forgive us
our sins and purify us from all unrighteousness."*
(1 John 1:9, NIV)

PERSONAL FELLOWSHIP (5-10 Minutes).

EVANGELISTIC PREPARATION (10-15 Minutes).

Briefly compare your experiences from sharing your personal testimonies this past week. Then practice giving your testimonies again. Seek to be brief, concise, and be sure to use Scripture. Remember to focus on *why* you became a Christian.

SHARING FROM YOUR SPIRITUAL JOURNALS
(10-15 Minutes).

A. Exchange insights from your SJ—QT and SN highlights.

B. Share your previous SM verses and discuss any insights received from meditating on this week's new verse.

DISCUSS APPENDIX F – A BIBLE STUDY METHOD

Take turns reading paragraphs together audibly, stopping to emphasize points as you feel led.

BIBLE STUDY DISCUSSION (10-15 Minutes).

A. Discuss your LCD, Lesson 6, *God Our Father*.

TOPICAL READING DISCUSSION (5-10 Minutes).

Discuss highlights from your reading of *Confession*, Chapter 6. Supplement your discussion with page 11 of your SJ.

PRAYER TIME TOGETHER (5-10 Minutes).

Spend this time in silent prayer confessing and forsaking any sin that's keeping you from effective Christian living.

WEEKLY SPIRITUAL GROWTH ASSIGNMENT #7
(5 Minutes).

1. Continue your daily QTs, praying to be an empowered witness! Be prepared to share your favorite personal insights next week.
2. Pray specifically for opportunities to share a word of truth or your testimony with someone who needs Christ.
3. Take sermon notes using your SJ. Be prepared to review highlights during your next meeting.
4. Complete Lesson 7 in the LCD.

5. Read TG, Chapter 7, *Sharing God's Plan of Salvation*. Mark highlights as you read. Be prepared to start sharing the Bridge Illustration during the next session. Practice presenting one verse at a time with explanation before moving on to the next verse. To aid with retention, number the presentation steps in your book.

6. Memorize the *Sinner's Prayer* included in your Scripture memory cards. Be prepared to share it next week.

During this coming week, prayerfully plan to meet together and complete the *Spiritual Application Project* of your choice.

SESSION SEVEN DISCIPLER'S PREPARATION MATERIAL

"And He died for all, that those who live should no longer live for themselves but for Him who died for them and was raised again." (2 Corinthians 5:15, NIV)

MOTIVATION FOR EVANGELISM (20-25 Minutes).

Read Acts Chapter 4 out loud together, stopping for discussion. Emphasize the boldness that Peter and John experienced through the power of the Holy Spirit. Point out that the same Holy Spirit is living in us at this very moment and wants to give us the same boldness! Remind your Timothy that Peter and John were no different from us. They chose to be obedient and yielded their lives to be used as instruments in the hands of a powerful, loving God who yearns for all men to come to Him. 2 Peter 3:9 says *"The Lord is patient, not wishing for any to perish but for all to come to repentance."*

SHARING FROM YOUR SPIRITUAL JOURNALS
(10-15 Minutes).

A. Exchange insights from your SJ—QT and SN highlights.

B. Share the *Sinner's Prayer* with one another.

C. Read and discuss Appendix G. Take turns reading aloud and emphasize key points as you read.

TOPICAL READING DISCUSSION (25-30 Minutes).

A. Discuss the highlights of TG, Chapter 7, *Sharing God's Plan of Salvation.*

B. Present the Bridge Illustration to one another. If your Timothy is having a problem explaining the entire "bridge," ask him to practice presenting one verse from the bridge successfully before moving to the next.

BIBLE STUDY DISCUSSION (10-15 Minutes).

Discuss your LCD, Lesson 7, *The Ministry of the Holy Spirit.*

PRAYER TIME TOGETHER (5 Minutes).

Pray for opportunities to share the "bridge" this week.

WEEKLY SPIRITUAL GROWTH ASSIGNMENT #8
(5 Minutes).

1. Practice presenting the Bridge Illustration with a Christian friend this week.
2. Continue your daily QTs, praying to be an empowered witness! Be prepared to share your favorite personal insights next week.
3. Take sermon notes using your SJ. Be prepared to review highlights during your next meeting.

4. Memorize **PSALM 119:11** and meditate on this verse. Be prepared to share your verses next week.
5. Complete Lesson 8 in the LCD.
6. Read TG, Chapter 8, *Petition*. Mark meaningful highlights and come prepared to discuss them next week.

SESSION EIGHT DISCIPLER'S PREPARATION MATERIAL

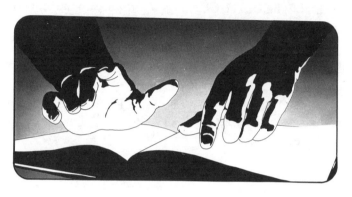

"Until now you have not asked for anything in My name. Ask and you will receive, and your joy will be complete." (John 16:24, NIV)

INFORMAL CONVERSATION (5-10 Minutes).

BRIDGE ILLUSTRATION PRACTICE (10-20 Minutes).

DISCUSS LAST WEEK'S DEVOTIONAL ASSIGNMENTS
(10-15 Minutes).

A. Exchange insights from your SJ—QT and SN highlights.

B. Share your previous SM verses and discuss insights you received from meditating on this week's verse.

DISCUSS LAST WEEK'S BIBLE STUDY ASSIGNMENT
(10-15 Minutes).

Discuss your LCD, Lesson 8, *The Importance of God's Word.*

DISCUSS LAST WEEK'S READING ASSIGNMENTS
(5-10 Minutes).

Discuss the highlights of TG, Chapter 8, *Petition.* Supplement your discussions with page 10 of your SJ.

PRAYER TIME TOGETHER (5-10 Minutes).

Together, write down your three most urgent personal needs in the special prayer section of your *Spiritual Journal.* Pray together for both of your needs.

WEEKLY SPIRITUAL GROWTH ASSIGNMENT #9
(5 Minutes).

1. Share the Bridge Illustration with a non-Christian this week.
2. Continue your daily QTs, praying to be an empowered witness! Be prepared to share your favorite personal insights next week.
3. Take sermon notes using your SJ. Be prepared to review highlights during your next meeting.
4. Memorize **2 CORINTHIANS 5:17** and meditate on this verse. Be prepared to share your verses next week.
5. Complete Lesson 9 in the LCD.
6. Read TG Chapter 9, *Giving is Worship.* Mark meaningful highlights and come prepared to discuss them next week.

During this coming week, prayerfully plan to meet together and complete the *Spiritual Application Project* of your choice.

SESSION NINE
DISCIPLER'S
PREPARATION
MATERIAL

9

"Then celebrate . . . by giving a freewill offering in proportion to the blessings the Lord your God has given you."
(Deuteronomy 16:10, NIV)

INFORMAL CONVERSATION (5-10 Minutes.

BRIDGE ILLUSTRATION PRACTICE (10-15 Minutes).

DISCUSS LAST WEEK'S DEVOTIONAL ASSIGNMENTS
(10-15 Minutes).

A. Exchange insights from your SJ—QT and SN highlights.

B. Share your previous SM verses and discuss insights you received from meditating on this week's verse.

C. Relate your experience(s) of sharing the Bridge Illustration with a non-Christian this week.

DISCUSS LAST WEEK'S BIBLE STUDY ASSIGNMENT (15-20 Minutes).

Discuss your LCD, Lesson 9, *The Church — A Supportive Fellowship.*

DISCUSS LAST WEEK'S READING ASSIGNMENTS (15-20 Minutes).

A. Discuss the highlights of TG, Chapter 9, *Giving is Worship.* If you are not experiencing joy and obedience in this area of your life, make a commitment with the Lord to start this week. Purpose to be a good example to your Timothy. *"The things you have learned and received and heard and seen in me, practice these things; and the God of peace shall be with you."* (Philippians 4:9)

B. Open your Bibles together. Ask your Timothy to read 2 Corinthians 9:6 & 7 and share what this verse means to him.

C. Share your personal testimony on giving by explaining *why, when* and *how* the commitment was made, plus how God has blessed it.

D. Ask your Timothy if he has a plan for giving. If he doesn't, help him develop one. Be sure to emphasize faith and joy!

PRAYER TIME TOGETHER (5 Minutes).

Pray for your church and for joyful obedience in giving.

WEEKLY SPIRITUAL GROWTH ASSIGNMENT #10
(5 Minutes).

1. Continue your daily QTs, praying to be an empowered witness. Be prepared to share your favorite personal insights next week.
2. Take sermon notes using your SJ. Be prepared to review highlights during your next meeting.
3. Memorize **1 JOHN 5:13** and meditate on this verse. Be prepared to share your verses next week.
4. Read TG, Chapter 10, *Thanksgiving*. Mark meaningful highlights and come prepared to discuss them next week.
5. Pray for opportunities to share Christ this week.
6. Enjoy personal independent Bible study by following the steps outlined in Appendix F. Be ready to share your favorite insights next week. Please note the importance of the genealogy, history, and Biblical background for this study.

SESSION TEN
DISCIPLER'S
PREPARATION
MATERIAL

". . . give thanks in all circumstances, for this is God's will for you in Christ Jesus." (1 Thessalonians 5:18, NIV)

INFORMAL CONVERSATION (5-10 Minutes).

DISCUSS LAST WEEK'S DEVOTIONAL ASSIGNMENTS (15-20 Minutes).

A. Exchange insights from your SJ—QT and SN highlights.

B. Share your previous SM verses and discuss insights you received from meditating on this week's verse.

C. Practice sharing your personal testimony or the Bridge Illustration with one other.

DISCUSS LAST WEEK'S BIBLE STUDY IN MATTHEW
(15-20 Minutes).

Share the insights which you both discovered as you studied Matthew, Chapter 1. Make sure that your Timothy took time to pray and personally apply each truth discovered.

DISCUSS LAST WEEK'S READING ASSIGNMENTS
(10-15 Minutes).

Discuss the highlights of TG, Chapter 10, *Thanksgiving*. Supplement your discussion with page 12 of your SJ.

LIFESTYLE EVANGELISM

Discuss the importance of being faithful as an empowered witness! Focus on all three ways of witnessing and the progress that has been made. Challenge one another to:

- Pray daily for the opportunity to witness.
- Follow-up those whom you reach.
- Set an example by the way you live.

INVITATION TO CONTINUE IN *A CALL TO MINISTER:*

Congratulate your Timothy on having completed his *A Call To Growth* training and if *A Call To Minister* is available, invite him to continue with you into the third and most advanced segment of discipleship training. The church may want to have a public recognition of your Timothy's having completed *A Call To Growth* during a worship service in the near future. *A Call To Growth* certificates are available in packs of ten.

PRAYER TIME TOGETHER (5 Minutes).

Take turns praying for one another's walk with God and the ministries God has for you in the future.

WEEKLY SPIRITUAL GROWTH ASSIGNMENT #11
(5 Minutes).

1. Continue daily Quiet Times and sermon note-taking using your SJ. When you finish the *Quiet Time Readings* in Appendix A, start in Matthew using the Bible reading schedule on page 88 at the back of your SJ.

2. Memorize **JOHN 10:28** and meditate on this verse. You will want to have an expanded memory system so you can continue memorizing Scripture consistently. *Scripture Memory Packets* (52 weeks) and the *Victory Scripture Memory Booklet* series (26 weeks each book) are available. (See TG page 257 for these resources).

3. Study Appendix H and mark the approaches you feel most comfortable using in the future.

APPENDIX 1
DEALING WITH
TEMPTATION

A CHARACTER BUILDING PROJECT

A. Read together 1 Corinthians 10:13.

B. Discuss with your Timothy the strongest temptation which he struggles with in his daily life.

C. Discuss definitions and key verses:

1. *Trials* – circumstances in life used by God to mature us as we learn that we can trust Him in all situations (Romans 8:28 & 29).

2. *Temptations* – sinful acts we consider doing which have the potential, if carried out, of hindering our spiritual growth and causing us to deviate from God's will (James 1:14, 1 Peter 5:8).

3. *Sin* – willfully doing wrong by breaking God's commandments; seeking pleasure and fulfillment in disobedience rather than in Him (John 14:21, 1 John 3:4).

D. Background Study: The same Greek root word is translated
    both *trial* and *temptation*. The context must dictate the proper
    translation. Example: "Blessed is the man who perseveres under
    trials...let no one say when he is *tempted*..." (James 1:12 & 13).

E. Emphasis of Study: We must plan in advance to overcome
    temptation.

F. Discussion: Provide the following references, insights, and
    questions, asking your Timothy to make personal application.

JOSEPH

REFERENCE: Genesis 39:1-9

INSIGHTS:

1. Joseph was in a position of trust, and therefore exposed to
    greater temptation.

2. He refused to sin because he valued his relationship with
    God more than pleasure.

3. He fled from temptation because of his prior spiritual
    commitment.

QUESTIONS:

1. Does "radical" accurately describe Joseph's actions?

2. As the Discipler, relate how God has most recently enabled
    you to successfully deal with a personal temptation (2 Peter
    2:9a).

JESUS

REFERENCE: Matthew 4:1-11

INSIGHTS:

1. Jesus was tempted, though He was Spirit-controlled.

2. His spiritually-significant baptism was followed by severe temptation.

3. The type of temptation He experienced was related to His capabilities.

4. His confident attitude reflected his understanding that our enemy has limited power, is a deceiver, and will ultimately be defeated.

QUESTION:

1. In following Jesus' example, what personal steps should be taken in regard to: building strong convictions, acquiring spiritual disciplines, understanding Satan's nature, and developing confidence in God's adequacy?

CHARACTER DEVELOPMENT

Plan ahead to defeat a specific temptation (Philippians 4:13).

PRACTICAL HELP

A. If he yields to immoral thoughts, find out what sort of literature or movies he is exposed to.

B. Show him some good verses to memorize concerning his area of weakness.

C. Check with your Timothy to see if he is *fleeing* from those situations which aggravate the temptation.

A CHARACTER BUILDING PROJECT:

A. Prayerfully present the teaching in 2 Timothy 2:20 & 21. Emphasize the words *if* and *cleanse yourself.*

B. Present and briefly discuss the following:

 1. Temptation itself is *not* a sin.

 2. To know God does not *eliminate* temptation.

 3. Temptation *maximizes* the pleasure and *minimizes* the consequences of sin.

 4. The way we *respond* to temptation *reveals* our true character and convictions.

 5. *Emotions* seek to overcome *knowledge* during a period of temptation.

 6. The key to victory is *choosing* rather than *wishing* to overcome temptation (James 4:7 & 8).

C. Present and discuss these verses and statements describing what happens when you yield to temptation:

 1. Temporarily, you reject Christ's Lordship, so you forfeit the benefits of His guidance (Proverbs 3:5 & 6).

 2. You become insensitive to the Holy Spirit's correction and teaching (Hebrews 3:13-15).

 3. God chastises you because He loves you (Hebrews 12:5 & 6).

4. God chooses not to answer your prayers (Psalm 66:18).

5. Your fellowship with God is hindered (1 John 1:5-7).

6. You open other areas of your life to attack from Satan. See David (2 Samuel 11:11-15).

7. Future temptation becomes harder to resist. See Samson (Judges 16:1, 4, 5, 15-17, 20, 21).

8. Your willingness to compromise encourages others to continue to sin. See Aaron (Exodus 32:1-8).

9. You may finally forfeit the privilege of being a spiritual leader. See King Saul (1 Samuel 13:13 & 14).

10. You may endanger your life by underestimating God's holy hatred of sin (Proverbs 29:1, 1 Corinthians 5:1-5). See Ananias and Sapphira (Acts 5:1-10).

D. Discuss insights and questions:

REFERENCE: 1 Corinthians 10:13, James 4:7 & 8

INSIGHTS:

1. Other people encounter the same temptations we do.

2. God is faithful; and through His enabling power there is no temptation which we cannot overcome.

DISCUSSION QUESTIONS FOR APPLICATION:

A. How have you personally chosen to resist the Devil by drawing near to God when tempted during the last two weeks?

B. How and when did God show you His way of escape? Share practical, personal examples.

C. The most helpful insight I have gained from this study is...

Pray about making personal application of that new or renewed insight. It must move from *insight* to *conviction* to become a *commitment*!

SPIRITUAL
APPLICATION
PROJECTS

1 – 5

CREATING A CONSCIOUS AWARENESS OF THE LOSTNESS OF MAN

1

"I have great sorrow and unceasing anguish in my heart. For I could wish that I myself were cursed and cut off from Christ for the sake of my brothers. . ." (Romans 9:2 & 3, NIV)

Evangelism is accomplished by people not programs. It isn't often achieved by simply giving a person a piece of literature, and hoping that he or she will follow the directions. Behind effective ministry, there is always *someone* who prays and cares! That someone has experienced the life-changing power of God, and has determined to become a channel of blessing to others.

Merely *telling* your Timothy about witnessing is not enough. Challenging him to *pray* for life's greatest opportunity is step number one. Next, you need to take him *with you* and let him observe and experience evangelism. Remember, the vision for witnessing is not so much taught, as caught.

TRAINING FOR EVANGELISM

How can you create a conscious awareness of the lostness of man? Remember, this is a prerequisite for effective instruction in the life of your Timothy. You can begin by sharing Luke 10:2 and dramatizing its meaning with a real-life spiritual application project. Take him to your car and quietly say, "For the next few minutes, let's meditate on what we're going to see, let's look at the harvest."

Drive him slowly up and down the streets of his own city. Show him the nicest homes; take him to the slums; show him the business district; cover as much of his vineyard as possible. Show him the harvest! Lead him to the conscious awareness that God has given him *his own* mission field. Remind him that he does not live in his town or neighborhood by accident. God has graciously saved him and placed him here to be a faithful and empowered witness. Through faith and prayer, part of this city belongs to him: he is here to help win it to Christ in preparation for the Lord's victorious return.

If all new Christians were given the benefit of a tour like this, their eyes would soon be opened, and the Holy Spirit would break their hearts. They would begin to see the city as God sees it! Before long they would grow to understand the spirit of Jesus when he cried out, "O Jerusalem, Jerusalem . . . how often I have longed to gather your children together, as a hen gathers her chicks under her wings, but you were not willing." (Matthew 23:37)

Every Christian needs to have his or her heart broken over the lost condition of people. Most believers have never seen the harvest with spiritual eyes or been led to view their personal ministry in these terms.

When you return home after taking your Timothy on this drive, sit down and say, "Do you know that you and I are part of God's plan for reaching this city? We can participate in reaping this wonderful harvest." Then turn to the Scriptures and read Ephesians 2:8-10 together: "For it is by grace you have been saved, through faith — and this is not from yourselves, it is the gift of God — not by works, so that no one can boast. For we are God's workmanship, created in Christ Jesus to do good works, which God prepared in advance for us to do." Then say to him: "Now John, by the grace of God, you and I have been saved for the specific purpose of doing the Lord's good work!" He said, ". . . and greater works than these will you do because I go unto my Father." (John 14:12)

Then explain that in the Bible, doing good works means having a personal ministry (Revelation 14:13). A good work is not merely a humanitarian effort, but is a God-inspired, and God-empowered act of spiritual service.

He needs to be gripped by this concept: "John, you were created and formed for a ministry that was prepared just for you. You have no idea how important you really are to God. He's got a special section of the harvest with your name on it."

It is essential for your Timothy to realize that he is unique and special. He is called to reap eternal *love* for God, for that is the true purpose of evangelism. He is to have a ministry that will produce beautiful fruit, and that fruit will remain forever.

It is *exciting* to challenge a fellow believer with this vision; then he can see that he is called to be a part of something that will last. To fulfill his life's mission and greatest purpose, he really has no choice but to do his special part in the Great Commission!

Robert Coleman has wisely said. "If your heart is to be gripped with a sense of destiny, you must see the value of your part in the strategy of God." As long as you are unaware of your part in God's strategy, whatever you do can seem insignificant and mundane. But when you realize that every single Christian has a vital role in God's plan, then you will have the incentive to accomplish all that God wants to do through your life.

You can conclude this inspirational session with your Timothy by saying something like this: "As your Discipler, it will be my privilege to pray with you and help you as you seek *your* ministry. My foremost desire is to help you become equipped to understand and then to do God's will. The Lord wants you to enjoy an abundant and fruitful life that pleases Him, so make it your constant goal to experience the highest and best purpose which He has for your service."

If you start out like this with your Timothy, then as he matures in his quiet time, Scripture memory, Bible study, character development, and other spiritual disciplines, he will naturally see their relationship to evangelism. With this balanced perspective, Satan will find it difficult to produce a dichotomy between spiritual growth and evangelism.

The deepest *motivation* for evangelism is love (Deuteronomy 6:5). Our *vision* is to see that the harvest is ready and become workers in it, praying that others will join us (Luke 10:2). God's *strategy* is spiritual multiplication (2 Timothy 2:2). The *participants* are fellow Christians who have been created and empowered to serve and bear witness (Ephesians 2:10 and Acts 1:8).

When you have led a person to know and love God, then you have produced fruit that will bring Him glory forever! Every time you lead someone to Christ and he starts loving God, you have produced the first natural fruit of the Spirit.

GIVING AN EVANGELISTIC BOOKLET AWAY

2

"And other seeds fell into the good soil and as they grew up and increased, they yielded a crop and produced thirty, sixty, and a hundredfold." (Mark 4:8)

If possible, plan to meet in a restaurant this week. Prayerfully seek to end the meal (the Discipler) by handing a booklet to the waitress and sharing a brief witness. Encourage your Timothy to do the same during your next meeting. Example: "This little booklet tells what it means to become a real Christian. Knowing Christ has been the best and most important decision of my life. He has given me peace, purpose and happiness! I know you are busy right now, but if you have any questions, my name and phone number are on the back." If the waitress expresses an interest and has time, you can briefly share your personal testimony.

If you cannot meet in a restaurant, consider other places where you could follow the same basic procedure. A drive-through fast food restaurant is an easy place to begin. The idea is to build confidence and develop a pattern of sincere concern.

During the coming weeks, you can take turns giving away booklets together. You can order additional evangelistic booklets as needed (See Resource Section at the back of the Timothy's Guide, page 257). We recommend; *Steps To Peace with God* and *Bridge To Life*.

Another good way of "sowing seed" is giving away all or a portion of the New Testament. Write an abbreviated personal testimony in the front along with your name and phone number. If you use the term "born again" in your testimony, include the page number from John chapter 3. If appropriate, you can paper clip an evangelistic booklet and a card from your church (preferably with a map on the card) on the inside flap of the Bible. This particular method will enable you to talk to someone and then ask, " would you like to have a free Bible to read?" When they receive it, they will also have your personal testimony, the Bridge Illustration booklet, your phone number, and a suggested place to worship.

Billie Hanks Jr. has worked closely with Word Inc. to develop an evangelistic audio-witness cassette entitled *Assured of Heaven*, so people can hear a clear presentation of the gospel while driving in their car or sitting at home alone. This is an effective witnessing tool which can be either given or loaned to a listener (See the Resource Section). You can briefly discuss this witnessing approach and list the names of two or three people who could best be reached by listening rather than by reading.

You can plan ahead to sow good seed by always carrying audio-witness cassettes, New Testaments and booklets in your car. New Testaments (NIV), may be purchased for only $2.10 (at the time of this printing) product # 01165 from The International Bible Society (800) 524-1588. They are a nonprofit organization that provide Bibles for evangelism at or below their cost.

The following true illustration shows how *one person* can make a lasting difference by simply sowing spiritual seed.

Frances Dixon, a Baptist preacher from England, once asked a young church leader named Peter to share his testimony about how he became a Christian. Peter said that while he was in the Royal Navy stationed in Sydney, Australia, he was walking down George street when he was stopped by a man with white hair. The man said, "excuse me, I wonder if I might ask you a question? I don't mean to offend you, but if you were to die today, where would you spend eternity? Would it be in heaven or would it be in hell? The Bible says it will definitely be in one place or the other. Would you give this your consideration? Good day." Peter said, "I'd never had anyone speak to me like that before. The question lingered in my mind, and when I went back to England, I found a church and asked the pastor how to be sure I could go to heaven."

Three years later, while Frances Dixon was conducting a church revival, a man named Nowell told his story. During the Second World War he was stationed in Sydney, Australia, and was approached by a white-haired man who asked him, "Excuse me, young fellow, I don't want you to be annoyed, but if you were to die tonight, where would you spend eternity?"

Later, Nowell went to church, heard the Gospel for the first time, and invited Christ to come into his life. Peter, who happened to be at the meeting, said, "He's got my testimony," so after the meeting, they compared notes and discovered that it was the same man who had talked with them.

Frances Dixon went on to Adelaide to preach on personal evangelism and he told the story of Nowell and Peter. It seemed amazing that these two men were both saved as the result of the witness of the same white-haired man. As Dixon told the story, a man in the audience raised his hand and said, "I'm another. I was walking down George Street in Sydney when a white-haired man stopped me and asked me that same question. As a result, I found a friend who told me how I too, might accept Jesus as my Savior."

Later, when Frances Dixon held a revival service in Perth and related the testimony of these three men, a deacon in the church came to him and said, "I was in Sydney one day walking down George Street, when a white-haired man asked me the same question and went on his way. I knew I had to settle the matter, so I found a church where the pastor told me how I could accept Jesus Christ as Savior and Lord."

Wherever he went, even in places as far away as Jamaica and India, Rev. Dixon met people whose lives had been touched by this white-haired man — eight in all. While he was in India speaking at a missions conference, one of the older missionaries said, "I am another. I too was approached by the old white-haired man and as a result I asked Christ to come into my life."

Dixon was determined that if given the chance, he would someday meet this faithful witness for the Lord. Finally, on his way home from a ministry tour, he stopped in Sydney and looked up a Christian friend. He asked him, "Do you know of a white-haired man on George Street who stops people and asks, "'If you were to die today, where would you spend eternity?'" Dixon's friend replied, "Sure, that would be Mr. Jenner." The two men went to Mr. Jenner's humble cottage, where Frances told the old man of his travels over the world, and the many who had come to know Christ as the result of his witness. Mr. Jenner related that for the last 25 years he had approached at least ten people each day in the same manner. However, with tears in his eyes, he said, "I've never personally been privileged to pray with a person who has accepted Jesus Christ. I've just been a link in God's chain."

Frances Dixon shared his story with Gene Warr, a Christian layman who lives in Oklahoma City. Gene was speaking in a church when he related this story. A woman raised her hand and said, "I, too, was in Sydney, Australia, walking down George Street, and I invited Jesus into my life because of this same white-haired man."

Points for discussion:

- Every Christian can ask searching spiritual questions
- How powerful is the truth?
- How important is our faithfulness?
- What role does the Holy Spirit play in conviction and conversion?

"And He, when He comes, will convict the world concerning sin, and righteousness, and judgment." (John 16:8)

CONDUCTING AN EVANGELISTIC SURVEY

"We are therefore Christ's ambassadors, as though God were making His appeal through us. We implore you on Christ's behalf: Be reconciled to God." (2 Corinthians 5:20, NIV)

Think about the fruit of the Spirit; love, joy, peace, patience, kindness, goodness, faithfulness, gentleness and self-control (Galatians 5: 22 & 23). When we let the Holy Spirit empower us for witnessing, He gives us boldness and confidence together with the fruit of the Spirit (Acts 4:31). It is then, that God can use us in a dynamic way to effectively share the truth.

During this project, you and your Timothy can go to a mall or any available department or grocery store and conduct an evangelistic survey. Both of you will have clip boards with lined sheets of paper and will stand outside the store or mall at either side of the entrances. If you are at a mall with several entrances and exits, ask the survey question to people who are both entering and leaving. If you are at a grocery store, ask only people who are entering (by the time most people are finished grocery shopping, they are in a rush and less likely to participate).

As a person walks up, ask, "can you help us with a one question survey?" Most people will say "yes." Ask the question, "in your opinion, how does a person get to heaven?" Each time you ask a person this question, they are being confronted with the issue of eternity. You are actually sharing a word of truth. During a recent survey of 50 people in one hour, we found that 37% of the people answered said, "live a good life;" while only .05% of them said to accept Jesus Christ. The other 62.88% had responses such as "everyone goes to their own heaven," "there is no heaven," "following your heart," and "going to church." 4 people said, "I don't know." They were very open and we followed up by saying, "this little booklet by Billy Graham tells you how." We gave them a booklet with the church's business card stapled to the back.

If they continue in interest, ask them if they would like to see the Bridge Illustration. Turn your questionnaire over and share it with them. If you have a choice between going through a booklet or drawing the bridge, always draw the Bridge Illustration. It is more personable when they can view the truth blossom before their eyes. It is helpful if your church can print generic business cards so you can write your own name on the card. Each evangelistic booklet should have a card stapled to the back. The business card should also include a map showing the location of the church and service times. The people that didn't know how to get to heaven were really genuinely happy to receive the booklet. In a little over an hour, my Timothy got to share his testimony with a group of high school kids, I got to share my testimony with a lady, explain the Bridge Illustration and give away four evangelistic booklets. One lady shared that she had just had an abortion two days earlier and was struggling with how to deal with it.

A secondary benefit of the survey is that it will help you understand what the people in your culture think about heaven. One church is continuing this survey each week in different locations. This project will demonstrate how seriously lost your world is and will help you develop a greater burden for the lost people in your culture.

Most of the fish will swim through the net just like in Jesus' day. But, the Lord will catch a few fish if we will only put out the net. There will always be a few that "have ears to hear."

WRITING AN EVANGELISTIC LETTER

4

"My heart's desire and my prayer to God for them is for their salvation." (Romans 10:1)

Writing an evangelistic letter works particularly well when trying to share the Gospel with a relative or friend that lives out of town.

We suggest that you complete Spiritual Application #5 directly after this project.

BEFORE THIS SESSION

A. Photocopy pages 80 & 81 for your Timothy.
B. Read the following material and develop your own evangelistic letter.

DURING THIS SESSION

A. Emphasize the importance of sharing the Gospel with a relative or friend.

B. Discuss the unique advantages of writing an evangelistic letter:

1. It is personal.

2. It can be re-read.

3. You are able to say things that might be difficult in person.

4. The presentation is done without interruption.

5. The message can be presented in an orderly and clear manner.

6. Everyone enjoys receiving a letter.

STEPS TO WRITING AN EVANGELISTIC LETTER

The personal joy of finding Christ should be the most important part of this letter. Use normal terminology, avoiding words such as redemption, born again, and sanctification, unless he briefly explains the meaning of the words in the letter.

Present the following elements of the Evangelistic Letter.

1. A warm greeting.

2. Compliment the recipient on positive areas of his life.

3. Identify with a common need or event. Example: wedding, new child, loss of a loved one, loss of job, graduation, problems with children, divorce.

4. Seek to use appropriate verses about the plan of salvation. You may wish to draw the Bridge Illustration, or enclose an evangelistic booklet.

5. Include the sinner's prayer:

   • Lord Jesus, I am a sinner,
   • But I am sorry for my sins.
   • I want to turn from my sins. I am willing to begin a new life with Your help.
   • Lord Jesus, please come into my heart and life right now.

(You may photocopy this page only.)

- From this moment forward, my life belongs to You and You alone.
- I will love You, serve You, and tell others about You, and trust You to live Your life through me.
- Thank You Lord, for coming into my life and for forgiving my sins today.

6. Share your personal testimony in regard to receiving Christ and subsequent results. "Several years ago I committed my life to Christ..."

7. Encourage a decision. "If my letter has made sense to you, is there any reason why you should not receive Christ today?"

8. Express your continued interest and leave the door open for additional correspondence – "If you would like to discuss this further..."

As the Discipler, share your personal evangelistic letter. Point out the previously mentioned elements included in your letter.

Have your Timothy write an evangelistic letter to one of their selected relatives or friends. Encourage him to follow the previously discussed guidelines. Ask your Timothy to be prepared to share his letter at your next meeting.

DEVELOPING AN EVANGELISTIC STRATEGY

5

"I have become all things to all men, that I may by all means save some." (1 Corinthians 9:22)

We suggest that you complete Spiritual Application Project #4 before completing this project.

BEFORE THIS SESSION

A. Photocopy pages 84-90. Make a set for you and your Timothy.

B. Read the following material and complete your "Family Evangelism Chart," "Friend Evangelism Chart," and "Evangelistic Strategy." Sample charts are located on pages 87 & 89.

DURING THIS SESSION

A. Emphasize the importance of sharing the Gospel with a friend or relative.

B. After sharing your "Family Evangelism" and "Friend Evangelism " charts, have your Timothy complete his own charts.

C. Pray together and ask your Timothy to pick a person to share the Gospel with. Pray that the Lord will give him a genuine love and concern for this person.

D. Discuss the following questions regarding your Timothy's friend or relative. Encourage him to make notes on his chart as you discuss the following needs:

1. What "felt need" is this friend or relative experiencing? Example: insecurity, boredom, lack of purpose, guilt, loneliness, fear of death, poor self-image.

2. What is his current attitude? Example: rebellious, sentimental, cynical, indifferent, bitter, materialistic.

3. Is there a misunderstanding about Christianity? Example: It is: non-intellectual, a crutch, motivated by fear, based on works, a way— not the only way.

4. What is his greatest hindrance to knowing Christ; self-assurance, worship of job, immorality, scriptural ignorance, lack of conviction, confusion between religions, distrust of God?

5. What commonalities could lead to conversations about Christ? Example: Sports, hobbies, business, politics, illnesses, joys and family concerns.

BRIDGE BUILDING

A. As you develop an overall evangelistic strategy, consider the following options for developing a deeper friendship with your friend or relative.

1. Give him a phone call.

2. Invite him and his spouse to your home for dinner.

3. Send a favorite Christian biography, cassette, CD or video.

(You may photocopy this page only.)

4. Go out to lunch or dinner together.

5. Deliver a hot meal if he is sick.

6. Meet a physical need.

7. Send a birthday or get-well card.

8. Enroll in an exercise club together.

9. Attend a sporting event or movie together.

10. Offer to baby-sit, so he can have a night out with his spouse.

11. Play a sport together, (tennis, racquetball, basketball, etc.).

12. Go shopping together.

13. Invite him to a non-threatening church function.

14. Invite him to church.

15. Invite him to a Christian concert.

B. Ask your Timothy to write his own practical 6 month "Evange-listic Strategy" for leading his friend or relative to Christ. Ask him to be prepared to share it with you next week. Study Appendix H before implementing your strategy.

January – Begin daily prayer, asking God to convict him of his sin and spiritual need (John 16:8). Give him a phone call to see how he is doing.

February – Invite him and his spouse over for dinner. Share a word of truth. If he lives out of town, write a brief note that would include a word of truth or your favorite verse.

(You may photocopy this page only.)

March –   Attend a sporting event together. If he lives out of town, send a favorite Christian biography on a sports personality. Include a personal note on the inside cover. Send a birthday card.

April –   Ask him to go to lunch and share your personal testimony. Offer to watch his children so he and his spouse can enjoy a "night out." If he lives out of town, send a greeting card including your personal testimony.

May –   Ask him out to dinner and share the Bridge Illustration. Invite him to church. If he lives out of town, write the "Evangelistic Letter" described in Spiritual Application #4.

June –   Invite him and his spouse over to dinner for fellowship. If he lives out of town, write a follow-up letter.

If your friend or relative receives Christ, be sure you or someone follows him up.

Remember, Jesus said, "No one can come to Me, unless the Father who sent Me draws him." (John 6:44) It is our job to present the Gospel in a gentle and respectful manner (1 Peter 3:15). It is God's job to draw your friend or relative to Himself.

After developing an "Evangelistic Strategy," remain *consistent* and *flexible. Your first priority is always to be sensitive to the Holy Spirit's leading.* Feel free to alter your initial strategy as needed. Make sure your *walk* and *talk* are the same.

If your friend or relative rejects the Gospel at first, don't give up. Continue to show him just as much love and attention. Your friend or relative needs to realize that you aren't being his friend *just* so you can lead him to Christ. Sometimes, those who come the slowest, end up being the greatest disciples!

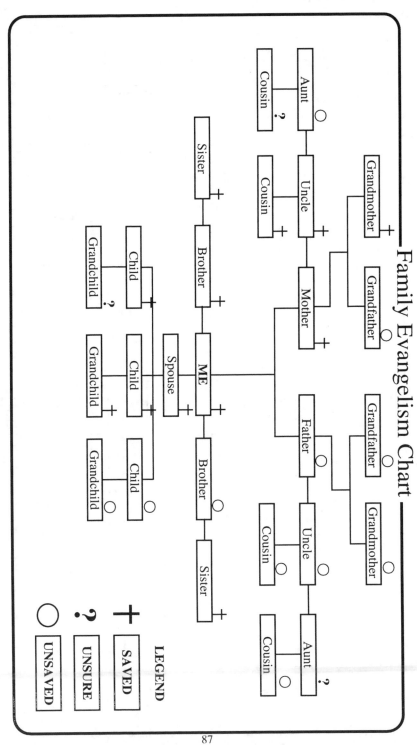

Family Evangelism Chart

(You may photocopy this page only.)

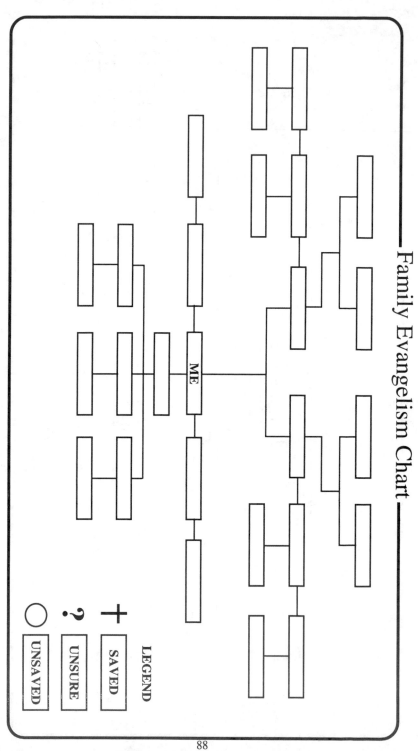

Family Evangelism Chart

ME

LEGEND

+ SAVED

? UNSURE

○ UNSAVED

(You may photocopy this page only.)

Friend Evangelism Chart

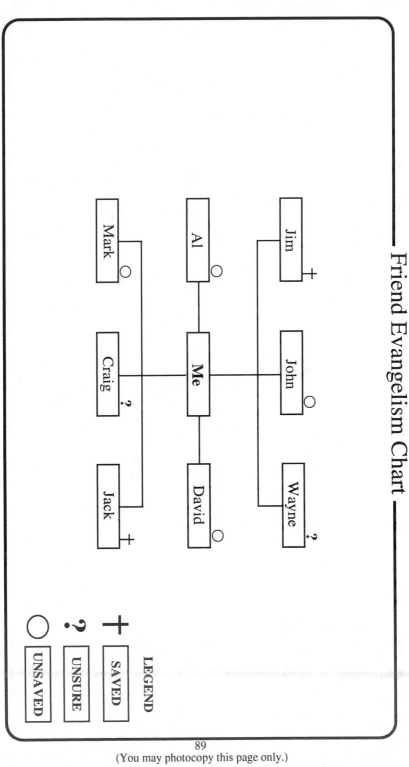

LEGEND

+	SAVED
•?	UNSURE
○	UNSAVED

(You may photocopy this page only.)

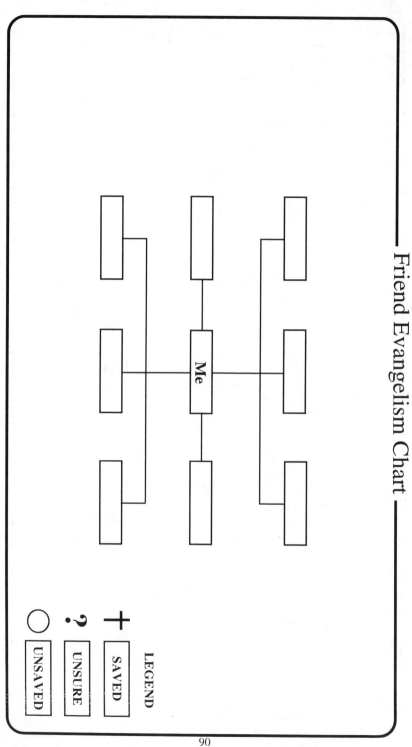

Friend Evangelism Chart

Me

LEGEND

+ SAVED

? UNSURE

○ UNSAVED

(You may photocopy this page only.)

ADDITIONAL NOTES

ADDITIONAL NOTES

ADDITIONAL NOTES

ADDITIONAL NOTES

ADDITIONAL NOTES

ADDITIONAL NOTES